THE
ILLUSTRATED
SURGEON
GENERAL'S
REPORT ON
CIGARETTE
SMOKING

PHOTOGRAPHS BY
ALFRED GESCHEIDT

WRITTEN BY
JACK GESCHEIDT

Published by Pomegranate Artbooks
Box 808022
Petaluma, CA 94975

Photographs © 1992 Alfred Gescheidt
Text © 1992 Jack Gescheidt

ISBN 1-56640-071-6
LC 92-60677

Designed by Harrah Argentine
Printed in Hong Kong

First Edition

■ DEDICATION

In loving memory of the original
Marlboro Man, who died years
ago from emphysema, and
whose beloved horse, Chemo,
was lost to passive smoke.

■ ACKNOWLEDGMENTS

SOME OF THE PEOPLE WHO APPEAR IN THIS BOOK:
Jack Barrick, Stanley Brooke, Colin Church, Andrew L.
Gescheidt, Jack Green, Stuart Hodes, Don Hudson,
Maurice King, Jacques Lowe, Bob Lyman, Mort Marshall,
Vincent C. Milone, Al Porte, Herman Vanderberg and
George Wendland.

SUGGESTIONS OR INSPIRATIONS:
Will Barnet, Ed Brown, Thomas F. Burke, Cornell Capa,
Howard Chapnick, Malvine Cole, George Dudley, John
Durniak, C. K. Eaton, Arthur Felig, Alan and Florence
Fisher, Martin and Marian Forscher, Richard Gilbert, Frank
Jacobs, Raymond Jonson, Ruth Lester, Bill Levison,
Howard Margulies family, Michael Perpich, Joan L. Schiff,
Rev. Bruce Southworth, Harry Sternberg, Arnold Wellman
and Howard Zieff.

TECHNICAL ADVICE AND OTHER ENCOURAGEMENTS:
Robert M. Cavallo, Dr. Stephen A. Cole, Dr. Gustave
Gordon, Dr. Stuart S. Leichter, Dr. Arnold Lisio, Marilyn
Mendelsohn, Eileen Perry, R.N., Dr. Sidney Printz, Dr.
Leslie Schiff, Dr. Russell Schiff and Dr. Louis Schneider.

PERSONAL INFLUENCES:
George Hoyningen-Huene, Alexey Brodovitch, Elizabeth
Timberman and Kurt Safranski. And to Lez Haas, who, at
the University of New Mexico in the 1940s, pointed me to
my life's profession.

My heart felt thanks to all.

SURGEON GENERAL'S WARNING:
Smoking May Be Hereditary.

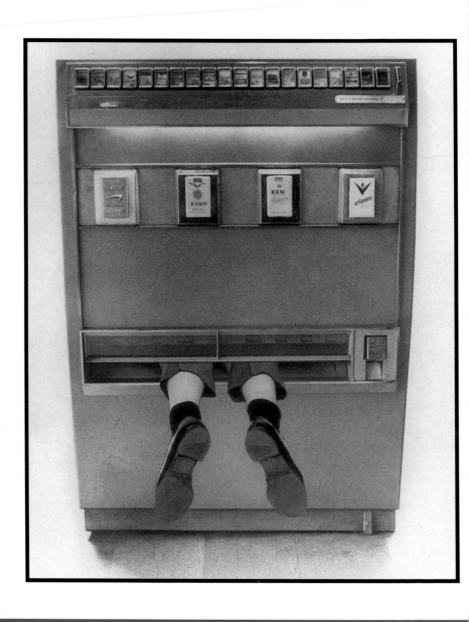

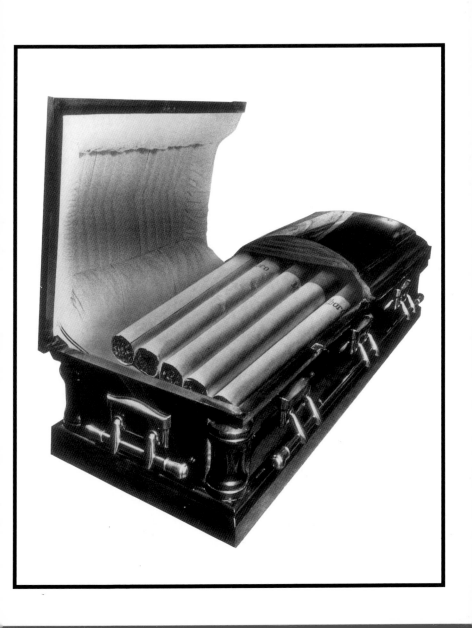

SURGEON GENERAL'S WARNING:
Don't Be Fooled by a Fancy New Flip-top Box.

SURGEON GENERAL'S WARNING:
Smoking Can Induce Weight Loss.

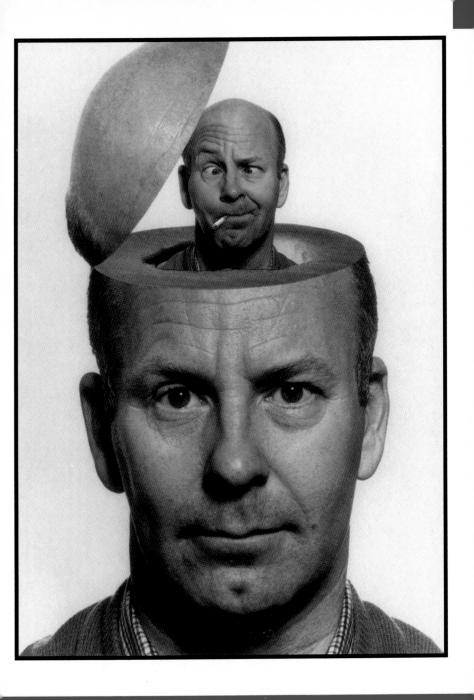

SURGEON GENERAL'S WARNING:
The Urge to Smoke Is All in Your Head.

SURGEON GENERAL'S WARNING:
Quitting Smoking May Produce Hunger Pangs.

SURGEON GENERAL'S WARNING:
Health Problems from Cigarette
Smoking May Be Irreversible.

SURGEON GENERAL'S WARNING:
Smokers Are Less Attractive to the Opposite Sex.

SURGEON GENERAL'S WARNING:
Some People Just Can't Quit.

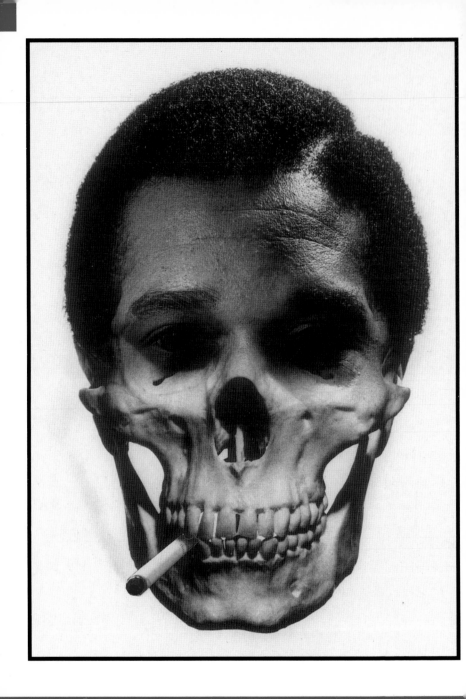

SURGEON GENERAL'S WARNING:
The Cigarette Industry Is an Equal
Opportunity Employer.

SURGEON GENERAL'S WARNING:
Smoking Can Cause Brain Damage.

SURGEON GENERAL'S WARNING:
You May Be in over Your Head.

SURGEON GENERAL'S WARNING:
Smoking May Stunt Your Horse's Growth.

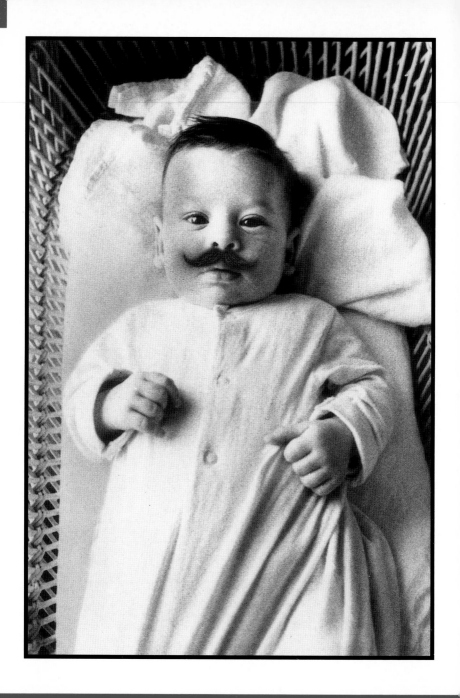

SURGEON GENERAL'S WARNING:
Smoking by Pregnant Women May Result in
Premature Maturity.

SURGEON GENERAL'S WARNING:
Future Generations Will Remember When
Smokers Roamed the Earth.

SURGEON GENERAL'S WARNING:
Studies Show Cigarette Smoking Is Addictive
to Laboratory Animals.

SURGEON GENERAL'S WARNING:
Smoking Increases Your Chances of
Catching Fire.

SURGEON GENERAL'S WARNING:
If You Must Smoke, Keep Your Cigarettes
at Arm's Length.

SURGEON GENERAL'S WARNING:
Smoking May Stunt Your Growth.

SURGEON GENERAL'S WARNING:
Stop Making an Ash of Yourself.

SURGEON GENERAL'S WARNING:
If Signs of Emphysema, Heart Disease and Lung
Cancer Don't Stop You, Maybe This Sign Will.

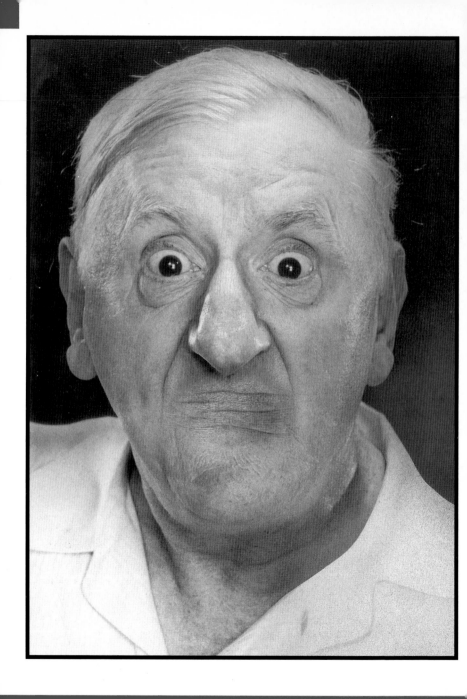

SURGEON GENERAL'S WARNING:
Some Cures for Smoking Do More
Harm Than Good.

SURGEON GENERAL'S WARNING:
Smoking by Pregnant Women Can Result in
Abnormal Child Development.

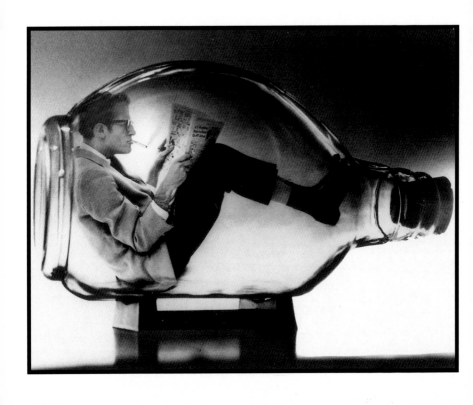

SURGEON GENERAL'S WARNING:
In the Future, Smokers Will Be Confined to
Smaller Smoking Areas.

SURGEON GENERAL'S WARNING:
Smoking May Cause Depression or
Disorientation.

SURGEON GENERAL'S WARNING:
Some Tobaccos Contain Minor Impurities.

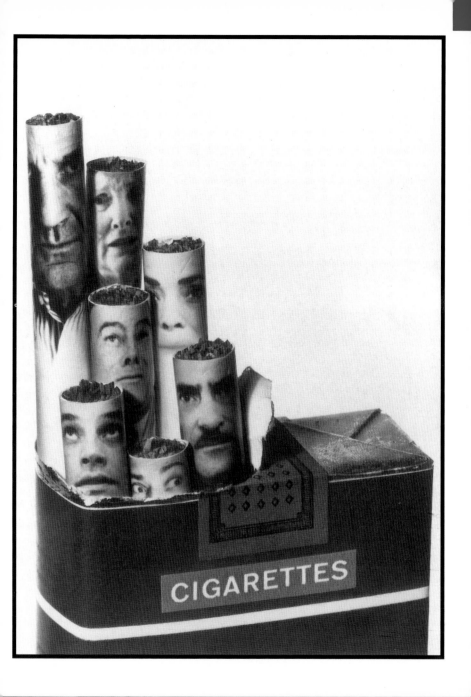

SURGEON GENERAL'S WARNING:
Don't Be Taken in by the Rest of the Pack.

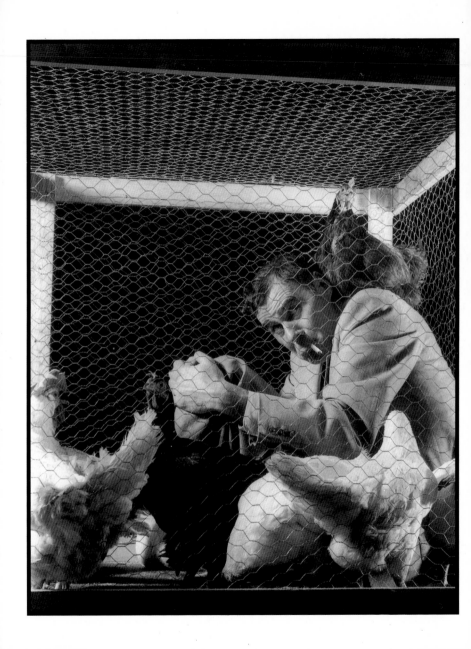

SURGEON GENERAL'S WARNING:
This Man Is Exhibiting the First Signs of
Nicotine Narcosis.

SURGEON GENERAL'S WARNING:
This Man Is Exhibiting the Last Signs of
Nicotine Narcosis.

SURGEON GENERAL'S WARNING:
Habitual Smokers May Require Psychotherapy.

SURGEON GENERAL'S WARNING:
Don't Be a Smart Ass.

SURGEON GENERAL'S WARNING:
Beware of Gimmicks
Offering Relief from Addiction.

SURGEON GENERAL'S WARNING:
A Cigarette Is Not a Toy.

SURGEON GENERAL'S WARNING:
Advertisers Will Do Anything to Reach
a Shrinking Market.

SURGEON GENERAL'S WARNING:
Refrain from Smoking While Handling
Delicate Instruments.

SURGEON GENERAL'S WARNING:
Smoking Is a Self-destructive Act.

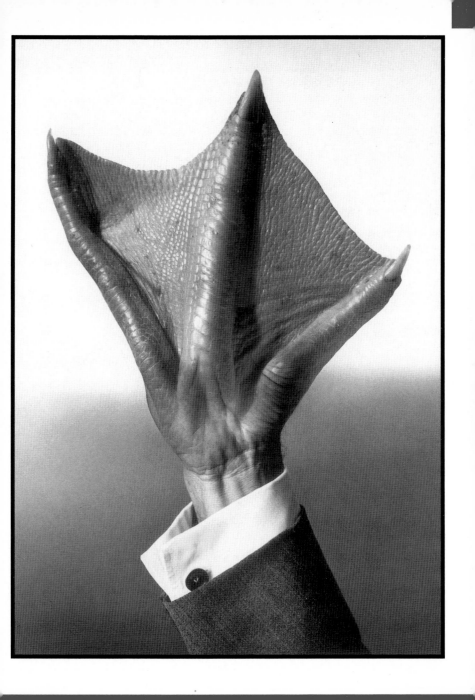

SURGEON GENERAL'S WARNING:
Cigarette Smoking May Cause Birth Defects.

SURGEON GENERAL'S WARNING:
Smoking Is Beneficial to Your Doctor's Health.

SURGEON GENERAL'S WARNING:
Quitting Smoking May Produce
Feelings of Anxiety.

SURGEON GENERAL'S WARNING:
Even One Cigarette Can Ruin Your Whole Day.

SURGEON GENERAL'S WARNING:
Quit Before Legislation Makes Cigarettes More
Difficult to Obtain.

SURGEON GENERAL'S WARNING:
Smoke and Your Image Will Suffer.